Sticky Note
Paper Airplanes

Sticky Note
Paper Airplanes

Steven H. Schmidt

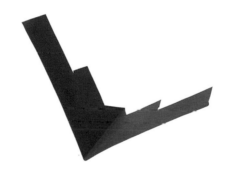

Sterling Publishing Co., Inc.
New York

Edited by Claire Bazinet
Design by Laura Case
Illustrations by Mario Ferro

Library of Congress Cataloging-in-Publication Data

Schmidt, Steven H.
  Sticky note paper airplanes / Steven H. Schmidt.
    p. cm.
  Includes bibliographical references and indcx.
  ISBN-13: 978-1-4027-2850-1
  ISBN-10: 1-4027-2850-6
  1. Paper airplanes. 2. Paper airplanes—Materials.
3. Sticky notes. I. Title.
 TL778.S3656 2006
 745.592—dc22

                                        2006007574

          2 4 6 8 9 7 5 3 1

      Published by Sterling Publishing Co., Inc.
      387 Park Avenue South, New York, NY 10016
            © 2006 by Steve Schmidt
      Distributed in Canada by Sterling Publishing
      c/o Canadian Manda Group, 165 Dufferin Street
          Toronto, Ontario, Canada M6K 3H6
  Distributed in the United Kingdom by GMC Distribution Services
Castle Place, 166 High Street, Lewes, East Sussex, England BN7 1XU
    Distributed in Australia by Capricorn Link (Australia) Pty. Ltd.
      P.O. Box 704, Windsor, NSW 2756, Australia

              Printed in China
              All rights reserved

      Sterling ISBN-13: 978-1-4027-2850-1
          ISBN-10: 1-4027-2850-6

For information about custom editions, special sales, premium and
corporate purchases, please contact Sterling Special Sales
Department at 800-805-5489 or specialsales@sterlingpub.com.

This book is dedicated to my two older brothers;

the three of us invincible in neighborhood park softball;...

and to my younger sister,

who knitted me a striped aviator scarf...

and then moved way too far away.

Contents

Foreword 11

Getting on the Flight Path . . . 13

Aeronautic Forces in Brief . . . 13

Paper Airplane Corollaries . . . 14

Design Categories 17

Launch Methods 19

Weight and Trim 20

The Planes 23

Sticky Note Classics 25
Dart 27
Flash Gordon 31
SST 35

Sticky Note Fold 39
U-Lite 41
X-Wing 45
Orbiter 47

Sticky Note Cut 49
F-15 51
Airfoil 55
Cylon 57
Vader 59
Diamondback 61
B-2 65
Swift 69
Cutlass 71

Sticky Note Two-Stage **75**

    V-Plane 77

    Reach 81

    Delta 85

    2 DI 89

        Wing Variations 92

Sticky Note Concepts **95**

    Simplex 97

    Manta 99

    Vector 103

A-12 107

Air Sled 109

Cruise 1 113

Condor 115

Spirit 119

Accessories 121

Ideas and Notes 123

Index 125

About the Author 127

Sticky Note
Paper Airplanes

Foreword

In this marvelous age of high-tech problem solving, it becomes necessary, on occasion, to step back from a particularly difficult problem. It makes sense to "take a breather," or "refocus," or "flush your mind"; whatever term you choose. In any event, a fresh perspective brought on by a brief diversion is always a welcome, even productive, course of action. Any really good manager realizes this.

A curious personal observation is that, as the magnitude of a problem increases on a linear scale, the magnitude of the diversion's ludicrousness increases exponentially. Sticky paper airplanes certainly fit into this pattern and have the additional benefit of presenting a new, albeit simpler, set of problems dealing with design, balance, and flight. The net result is that, all in one stroke, you have a diversion, a "breather," and a simple fun challenge that keeps your problem-solving skills active and sharp. Hell, anybody can make a paper airplane....

Getting on the Flight Path

Aeronautic Forces in Brief

Traditionally, there are four primary forces affecting an aircraft, as we know it, during flight (see Fig. A):

1. **Gravity** - the force working to pull the aircraft *down*.
2. **Lift** - the force generated by the wings as they move through the air, working to pull the aircraft *up*.
3. **Thrust** - the force generated by some type of engine, working to pull or push the aircraft *forward*.
4. **Drag** - the force generated by the airframe's *resistance* to being pulled or pushed through the air.

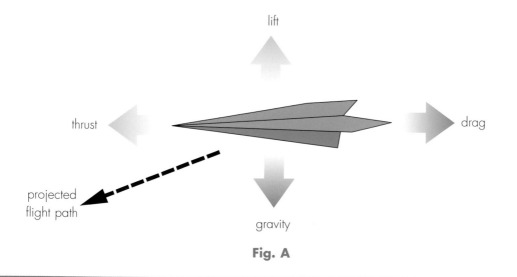

lift

thrust

drag

projected
flight path

gravity

Fig. A

We normally regard lift and thrust as **positive** forces while gravity and drag are **negative** forces. If the negative forces and the positive forces could cancel or equal each other exactly, they would be "balanced" kinetically, and we would have an aircraft remaining motionless in whatever position and altitude it was placed. By the application of thrust, one of the positive forces, we disrupt that kinetic balance. The reaction of the other forces, in their attempt to restore equality, results in forward and down-ward motion of the aircraft: flight.

There are other points to consider which include shape, material, and weight. These items are used to determine an aircraft's "physical balance." How well this information is assembled and implemented will determine how well the aircraft accomplishes flight. Literally any object can be made to fly if it is properly balanced "physically" and if its kinetic balance can be controlled.

Paper Airplane Corollaries

It is neither necessary nor smart to go much deeper into aeronautics to participate and enjoy paper airplane construction and performance. Paper airplane flight is simply a matter of fabricating a series of folds that channel airflow toward a single direction and then physically balancing the structure. The initial thrust is provided by hand launch. Artificial lift is generated by directed orderly airflow through the folded form. Gravity and drag are constant forces which draw the aircraft down. This group of events pulls the aircraft through the air mass. Air is channeled over and through the design, somewhat sustaining the artificial lift. At some point, a kinetic balance is established. That balance is constantly being altered by gravity and answered by generated lift. The result of this action is a controlled flight path.

Any paper airplane's ultimate flight path is down and forward. Generally, the better the design, the more "forward" is achieved in relation to descent. This is referred to as the aircraft's "glide ratio." Glide ratio is expressed as a numeric ratio (e.g., 4:1 or 4 units forward for every unit downward). A glide ratio of 20:1 means that the aircraft will go forward 20 feet for every foot of altitude it loses (pretty decent designwise). A glide ratio of .25:1, on the other hand, is forward motion of 3 inches for every foot lost in altitude; roughly the sink rate of, say, an empty intercity bus.

·········

There is another relationship that is important to keep in mind and that is the combination of the air, the size of the paper airplane, and the material (weight and strength) of which the paper airplane is constructed.

The air mass and density will remain constant for our purposes. This is an indoor diversion, so wind won't be a factor. The air mass will support an aircraft of a given size and weight. I don't think we have to worry about a

paper airplane that is too large, but we do have to worry about one that is too small.

If the aircraft is too small, its control surfaces will have no real meaning. It will have no directional control, no chance for kinetic balance and, consequently, will not "fly." Similarly, if we build an aircraft out of a large sheet of newspaper, it will be large enough to fly well and have ample control surface area but, while newspaper is light enough, it possesses absolutely no structural integrity. The aircraft will not maintain a defined form. The action of the aircraft's passage through the air mass will distort the craft's shape erratically on a moment-to-moment basis. Any kind of balance is then impossible. Consequently, so is flight.

As a side note, you now know why the paper airplane evolved so naturally with the standard bond (8½" by 11") typing paper. The size, weight, and strength

Needed Items

In order to build and fly the aircraft presented in this book, you will need:

1. a sticky note pad (3 inches square)
2. a sticky note pad (3 by 5 inches)
3. a few paper clips (various sizes)
4. a roll of office tape (preferably ¾-inch frosted)
5. a scissors
6. some imagination
7. some patience

Following the Folds

Although you may recognize in some illustrations certain symbols used in paper-folding arts, like dashed fold lines and curved arrows (see below), you don't need to know origami. Taken with the text, the art is self-explanatory and clearly marked. Simply follow the directions that lead in sequence from one drawing to the next, and you can't go wrong.

As in basic paper folding, creases should be made sharp and clean. If you're unsure of a fold, take a quick peek ahead to see what the resultant folds should look like. These basic origami techniques will help ensure more consistent and neater, hence more streamlined, fliers.

Basic folding symbols:

Dashed line - - - - - - - - - - - - - - - - - = fold forward/upward
Dashed and dotted line · - · - · - · - = fold backward/downward
Dotted line · · · · · · · · · · · · · · · = edge behind
Line ▶▶▶▶▶▶▶▶▶▶▶▶▶▶ with ✂ = cut here

factors of the paper, relative to the protected indoor air mass, lend themselves perfectly to the usual folded paper airplane designs.

· · · · · · · · ·

Okay, why sticky notes? Simple...

- The size promotes a smaller, challenging design field (3 x 3 or 3 x 5 doesn't take up much room).
- The paper weight is light and strong enough, yet the reduced size is still capable of yielding a good, stable aircraft.
- They're multicolored (easy to spot).
- The built-in adhesive helps to hold them together (eliminating some cumbersome structural folding).
- Every office has (or should have) sticky note pads everywhere.
- The planes build fast.
- They fly well.

Design Categories

The design portion of this book has been divided into five sections, or classes. The first, **Sticky Note Classics**, essentially covers *the* paper airplane most everyone knows and remembers. Its construction is a basic in/out fold, producing a split wing at the top of the design and a keel/rudder at the bottom (see Fig. B).

These are the classic "dart"-type paper aircraft.

·········

The second section, **Sticky Note Fold**, covers a design group similar to those in the first section, but makes use of the adhesive on the sticky notes to eliminate some folds and produce cleaner, more efficient designs (see Fig. C for example).

These are still "conventional"-type aircraft.

overhead view

overhead view

side view

Fig. B

side view

Fig. C

The third section, **Sticky Note Cut**, presents a group of designs that have one or two basic folds, but rely on strategic cuts to produce a particular shape or a control surface that would not exist in a plain-fold design (see Fig. D).

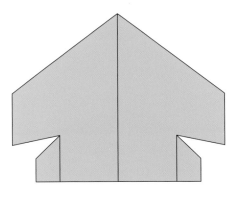

overhead view

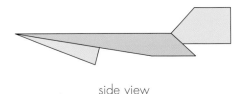

side view

Fig. D

These are "design evolution"-type aircraft patterned after American "X" and Century series fighters.

The fourth class, **Sticky Note Two-Stage**, is a novelty design group which combines more than a single sticky note sheet to produce different aircraft with features that wouldn't be possible in the single sheet format. The adhesive helps to form the wings, some joints, and keeps folds to a minimum. This two-stage category requires a bit more patience because the wings must be "fitted."

The fifth and final section, **Sticky Note Concepts**, stretches the imagination. It explores some nonconventional theories in support, wing configuration, and stability. It is the area of newness and freedom in aerodynamic paper airplane theory. Here I have included personally developed ideas like "air dams," anhedral wing planforms, and a design family I call the Manta series. I have "worked" on this type for a few years now.

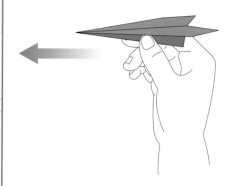

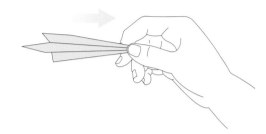

Fig. F

Fig. E

Launch Methods

All of the aircraft in this book are hand launched in one of three ways:

Method #1: Position the thumb and first finger on the lower fuselage, just behind the nose (see Fig. E).

The action is a forward, gentle snap.

Method #2: Position the aircraft nose and wing leading edge within the thumb and first two fingers, as shown in Fig. F.

The action is a level "pull" through the air. Or you can release upward (see Fig. G) for aerobatics.

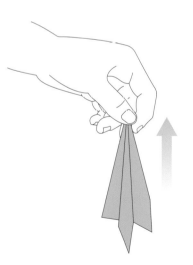

Fig. G

Method #3: Position the aircraft wing between the thumb and first finger at the rear of the plane (see Fig. H).

The action is a simple, gentle, guided push.

as possible. If you find there's too much weight forward, don't compensate by adding weight rearward; just remove some of the tape used forward or find a lighter weight paper clip.

. . . .

Trim will affect the aircraft's flight path. In almost every case, trim will be limited to bending the outer rear wing panels up or down, or bending the center of the rear wing up or down (see Figs. I and J).

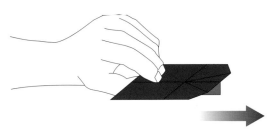

Fig. H

Weight and Trim

Weight is applied, generally to the nose section, to affect the aircraft's physical balance. Apply your office supply, ¾-inch cellophane tape in short strips as needed or attach a small paper clip. Each aircraft plan will show recommended starting weight and proper placement. It is desirable to keep the aircraft as light

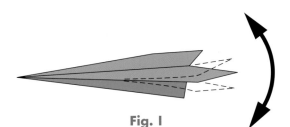

Fig. I

Fig. J

Viewing an aircraft from the rear...

- Bending the outer *right* wing panel down generally causes that surface to rise and the aircraft will bank *left*.
- Bending the outer *left* wing panel down will cause that surface to rise and the aircraft will bank *right*.
- Bending the outer *right* wing panel up will cause that surface to drop and the aircraft will bank *right*.
- Bending the outer *left* wing panel up will cause that surface to drop and the aircraft will bank *left*.
- Bending one outer wing panel up and the other down combines two control surfaces and will probably result in a violent bank in the direction indicated above. The aircraft will then spin rapidly.
- Bending the rear center *up* will cause the aircraft to nose *up*.
- Bending the rear center *down* will cause the aircraft to nose *down*.

You may cut definite control surfaces (see Fig. K) or simply bend edges.

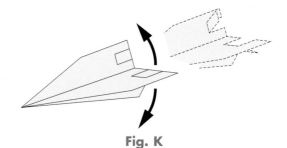

Fig. K

....

One method of "auto-trim" manifests itself in the way that the wing is folded. A paper airplane wing is seldom flat; i.e., at a 90° angle to the fusclage or "body" (see Fig. L). The wings are

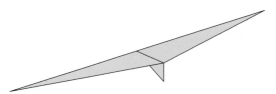

Fig. L

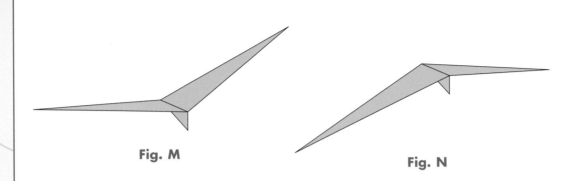

Fig. M

Fig. N

more often angled up, a property called **dihedral** (see Fig. M): and occasionally down, a property called **anhedral** (see Fig. N). Generally speaking, when an aircraft with dihedral enters a bank (turn), it wants to right itself or return to level flight automatically. It will tend to be more stable.

An aircraft with anhedral will *not* try to recover from a bank. Because of this fact, the anhedral aircraft is less stable and will spin out more easily. Although it is somewhat more difficult to balance, when it "works" the flight performance is absolutely deluxe.

It is most important to understand that weight and trim work together to provide kinetic balance. Understanding this relationship will mean the difference between "a little yellow thing" and a small-sized air vehicle that will amaze you with its flight performance.

THE PLANES

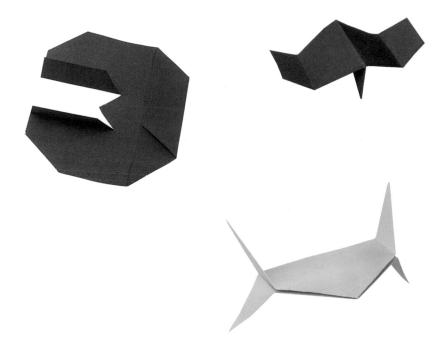

Sticky Note Classics

The following designs are the standard paper airplanes made since the onset of aeronautic daydreams. You will readily recognize them. In their usual letter-size form, they got us more visits to the principal's office than any other non-school-related activity. Their salient design features are a high wing and a pronounced dihedral over a keel fuselage. All three of these aircraft use the standard 3 x 3-inch sticky note and generally do not fly well. However, with proper weight and trim, the SST unit suddenly acquires excellent stability and becomes a great distance flyer. Relive your youth....

Dart ■ Flash Gordon ■ SST

Dart

— · — · —

Size: 3 x 3
Class: Classic
Type: Standard

Take a 3 x 3 sticky note with adhesive side up and find the centerline by folding to the back, as shown in Fig. 1-A.

Fig. 1-A

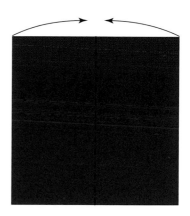

Lay the sheet flat and fold the corners inward on the dashed line (see

Fig 1-B). The adhesive will hold the folds.

Fig. 1-B

Next, fold the form in half toward the back, as shown in Fig. 1-C.

Fig. 1-C

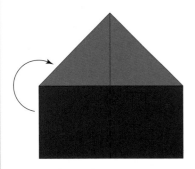

Rotate the form. The folded corners are now on the outside. Still viewing the aircraft from the side, on the dashed line, fold one wing toward you, as shown in Fig. 1-D.

Fig. 1-D

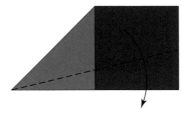

side view

Make an identical fold to the back in the other wing, as shown in Fig. 1-E.

Fig. 1-E

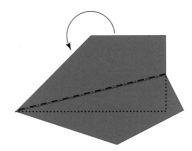

The result should look like Fig. 1-F, as viewed from the top. As shown, add some tape to the tip; about four pieces should do it.

Fig. 1-F

overhead view

The addition of tape will provide trim and serve to hold the wings together. Bend overlapping tape neatly around the wing leading edge. Make all folds and creases sharp. Finally, make sure the wings have a little dihedral, as seen from the front in Fig. 1-G.

Fig. 1-G

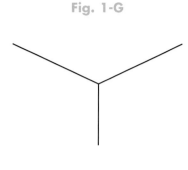

forward view

This aircraft flies just like the one you remember making in school; maybe a little better. Use launch method #1. Flight is stable, requiring little trim (provided you haven't badly stressed the paper during construction).

Flash Gordon

Size: 3 x 3
Class: Classic
Type: Schoolyard

Take a 3 x 3 sticky note sheet with adhesive side up. Find the centerline. With the sheet flat, as shown in Fig. 2-A, fold the corners on each side in to the center.

Fig. 2-A

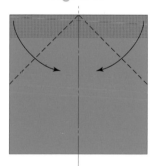

With the adhesive holding the folds in place, fold the tip forward. See Fig. 2-B on the next page.

Fig. 2-B

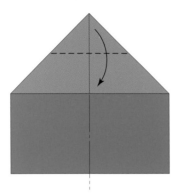

Turn the form sideways, as in Fig. 2-D, and fold the wings down, front and back.

Fig. 2-D

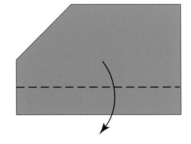

Fig. 2-E

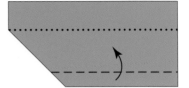

Fold the form in half on the centerline as shown in Fig. 2-C.

Previous folds are inside. Make sure all creases are sharp.

The folds form a shallow keel between the wings, as shown as dotted line in Fig. 2-E. Fold the ends of the side panels up along the dashed fold line.

Viewing the aircraft from the front, it should resemble Fig. 2-F.

Fig. 2-F

forward view

Fig. 2-C

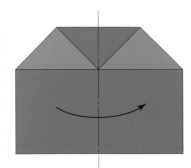

Place 3 to 4 small pieces of tape across the nose for physical balance.

You can simply bend the trailing edges of the wings up or down for flight trim or you can cut control panels and adjust them (see page 21).

Any one of the three launch methods can be used:

#1 will yield a fast aerobatic flight.

#2 will cause a loop and gentler aerobatics.

#3 will cause a longer, smoother flight.

· · · · · · · · ·

Originally folded using full sheets of typing paper, this aircraft flew well outdoors. Indoors, it was not a favorite...not with teachers, that is.

SST

Size: 3 x 3
Class: Classic
Type: Full Delta

Take a 3 x 3 sticky note sheet with adhesive side up. Find the centerline. With the sheet flat, fold as shown in Fig. 3-A, *across* the centerline.

Fig. 3-A

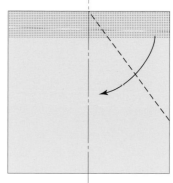

Fold the opposite corner as shown in Fig. 3-B. See Fig. 3-C for the resulting angle of the wing panels. The adhesive on the sticky note holds the crease.

Fig. 3-B

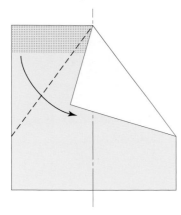

In Fig. 3-C, you are viewing the aircraft from the bottom. Fold it in half, to the back, along the centerline.

Fig. 3-C

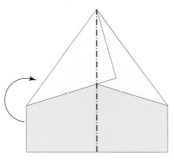

Lay the aircraft on its side and fold the top section forward, front and back, as shown by the dashed line (see Fig. 3-D).

Fig. 3-D

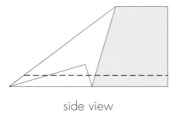

side view

The resulting fuselage, or keel, is very shallow (see

Fig. 3-E). Extend the wings outward and turn the aircraft so that you are viewing it from the top.

Fig. 3-E

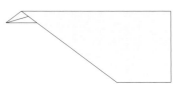

Apply two strips of tape to the nose as shown in Fig. 3-F. Fold the overlapping tape neatly over the leading edges of the wings.

Fig. 3-F

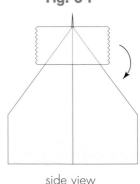

side view

The wings should have
have a slight dihedral,
as shown in Fig. 3-G.
Adjust trim as necessary
for level flight.

Fig. 3-G

forward view

Using launch method #1,
you will find this aircraft
to be one of the most
stable flyers in this
collection.

. . . .

Note: When I trimmed this
design, I found that the
control surfaces worked
opposite from the norm

(i.e., bending the right rear
surface up did not cause
the right wing to drop;
instead, the action that
resulted was that the right
wing rose). In the case of
this aircraft, the trim
works in reverse because
of the amount of wing
behind the swept leading
edge.

Sticky Note Fold

The following designs are also folded aircraft, but use both 3 x 3 or 3 x 5 sticky notes. They also make use of the adhesive band to eliminate certain folds and provide a greater wing area for flight. They are fair flyers and, once again, attention to weight and trim will significantly improve performance. One could probably achieve similar results with full-size sheets of paper and mucilage, but the sticky note versions are much easier...and there's no mess.

U-Lite ■ X-Wing ■ Orbiter

U-Lite

Size: 3 x 3
Class: Fold
Type: Gull Wing

Lay a 3 x 3 sticky note sheet with the adhesive upward. Fold it in half on the centerline. Spread the lower portion of the sheet apart until folds begin to appear as shown in Fig. 4-A.

Fig. 4-A

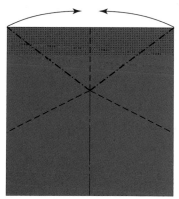

Bring the joined adhesive section down the sheet. Keep the tips together at the bottom centerline, as shown in Fig. 4-B, and neatly crease the side folds and complete the nose.

upper/lower wing surfaces together. Turn the aircraft sideways, as seen in Fig. 4-C, and add 2 or 3 pieces of tape to the keel as a starting balance point. The wings are level.

Fig. 4-D

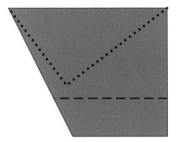

Fig. 4-B

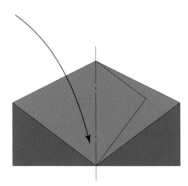

Fig. 4-C

side view

The fold is about one-third the distance of the wing span, as seen in Fig. 4-E.

Extend the wings out to the sides.

Make all the creases sharp. The aircraft is now lying top down with a deep keel facing up. The adhesive should be holding the keel and the

Now lay the aircraft on its side with its wings folded flat. As shown in Fig. 4-D, fold the wing on each side upward on the dashed line.

Fig. 4-E

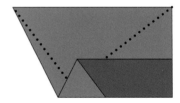

From the front, the aircraft should look like Fig. 4-F.

Fig. 4-F

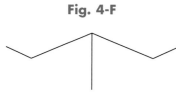

forward view

This aircraft works best with launch method #1 or #2. Method #1 should yield a simple straight flight; #2 will put the aircraft in an awkward position from which it will recover and continue on level.

Folding the wings in closer will raise the speed but lessen the stability. Extending the wings will reverse the conditions. Because the wing span is greater than the plane length, *watch the balance*. Balance the aircraft *before* you apply any trim controls.

X-Wing

Size: 3 x 3
Class: Fold
Type: Short Range

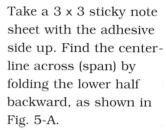

Take a 3 x 3 sticky note sheet with the adhesive side up. Find the center-line across (span) by folding the lower half backward, as shown in Fig. 5-A.

Crease sharply, then reopen and make similar creased folds on the diagonals shown by folding inward.

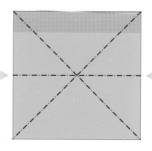

Fig. 5-A

Now collapse the span folds inward to form a triangle as in Fig. 5-B.

Fig. 5-B

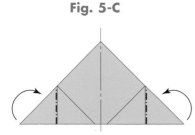

overhead view

There are actually two triangular sections, with the adhesive holding the upper one closed.

Fold the wing tips on the upper triangular section inward as shown in Fig. 5-C.

Fig. 5-C

Turn the aircraft over and do the same to the lower section. The aircraft will look like Fig. 5-D. Turn the aircraft back over (it will still look like Fig. 5-D) and add about 3 or 4 pieces of tape as shown. This will be a good starting balance point.

Fig. 5-D

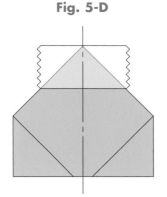

Bend the tape overhang down and around the wing leading edge. Open the wing tip folds to obtain the form shown in Fig. 5-E.

Fig. 5-E

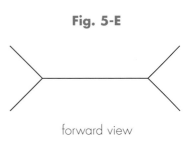

forward view

The launch method will be #3. This is a fast, straight flyer. Balance the aircraft first. You may then have to add in a little "up" elevator in the rear. Once trimmed properly, you can approach the "Death Wastebasket" as good as any star pilot.

Orbiter

Size: 3 x 5
Class: Fold
Type: Complex Delta

Take a 3 x 5 sticky note sheet with adhesive side up. Find the centerline but *do not* crease. Make two inward folds as shown in Fig. 6-A.

Fig. 6-A

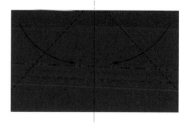

Note, in Fig. 6-B on the next page, that the two folds produce a wide nose and do not touch the centerline. Make the creases sharp. The adhesive will secure the folds.

Fig. 6-B

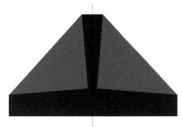

Turn the aircraft over. Fold the wings forward on the lines shown in Fig. 6-C.

Fig. 6-C

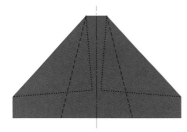

Now go to the wing tips and fold them toward the back on the fold lines, as shown in Fig. 6-D. Add 3 or 4 strips of tape to the nose and fold it under as a starting balance point.

Fig. 6-D

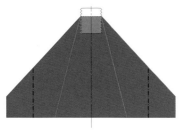

Adjust the wings so that the aircraft looks like Fig. 6-E from the side and Fig. 6-F from the front.

Fig. 6-E

side view

Fig. 6-F

forward view

Using launch method #3, send the aircraft forward. Once it is trimmed so that it does not dive or stall (porpoise), roll stability can be controlled by raising or lowering the rear of the outer wing panels. Properly trimmed, this aircraft flies slow and stable with a fairly high glide ratio.

Sticky Note Cut

The following designs use both 3 x 3 and 3 x 5 sticky note sheets. They utilize the adhesive band for minimum folds and then strategic areas are cut away. These cuts exemplify weight savings, design features, different wing configurations, and different weight distributions. One design actually has a real airfoil. Flight performance varies, but in general all of these designs fly well. Weight and trim will be a bit more critical for really good flights. Just pay attention.

F-15 ■ **Airfoil** ■ **Cylon** ■ **Vader** ■ **Diamondback** ■ **B-2** ■ **Swift** ■ **Cutlass**

F-15

Size 3 x 3
Class: Cut
Type: Short Sweep

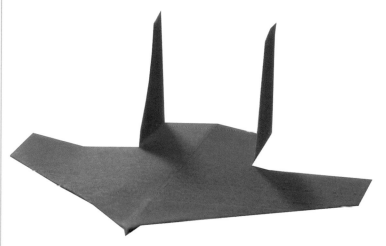

Take a 3 x 3 sticky note and find the centerline. Lay the note flat with the adhesive side up and bring the corners forward, as shown in Fig. 7-A.

Fig. 7-A

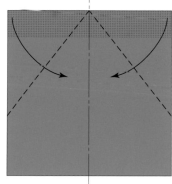

Join the tips with the adhesive, then expand that join over the centerline. As seen in Fig. 7-B, the outer folds should reach over halfway down the sides. Make the creases sharp.

Fig. 7-B

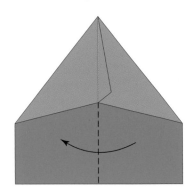

The aircraft is lying top down with a short keel facing up. The adhesive should be holding the keel and the upper/lower wing surfaces together. Fold the wings together on the centerline, keel inside. With the aircraft sideways, as in Fig. 7-C, cut through *both layers* of the wing as shown.

Fig. 7-C

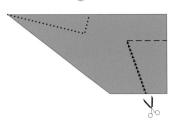

side view

Open the wings and fold up the "rudders" as in Fig. 7-D. Start with 3 or 4 pieces of tape over the nose for balance. Fold

down to conform with wing leading edge. Always balance the aircraft *before* you apply any trim controls.

Fig. 7-D

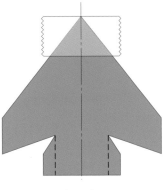

overhead view

Adjust the wings and rudders so that the aircraft looks like Fig. 7-E from the front.

Fig. 7-E
forward view

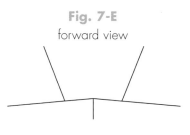

This aircraft works well with launch methods #1, #2, or #3. #1 or #3 should yield a simple straight flight. #2 will put the aircraft in an awkward position from which it will recover if balanced correctly.

Airfoil

Size: 3 x 3
Class: Cut
Type: Shaped Wing

Lay a 3 x 3 sticky note sheet with the adhesive side up, as in Fig. 8-A. Fold the adhesive section forward and crease at the fold line.

Fig. 8-A

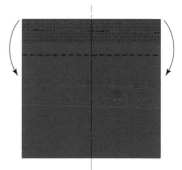

Complete the leading edge of the wing by leaving a little gap between the double layers, as shown in

Fig. 8–B, before sealing the adhesive.

Fig. 8-B

side view

Fig. 8-C is a view of the aircraft from the top.

Fig. 8-C

overhead view

Next, make two cuts, as shown in Fig. 8-D, and fold the cut sections upward on the dashed lines to serve as rudders.

Fig. 8-D

There is no dihedral or anhedral. The wing should be straight across, as shown in Fig. 8-E.

Fig. 8-E

forward view

Using launch method #3, send the aircraft forward and trim as necessary for level flight. Correctly balanced, this aircraft flies fast and stable. If the aircraft should dive, you may need to adjust the paper clip *and* add in some "up" elevator.

Cylon

Size: 3 x 3
Class: Cut
Type: Saucer

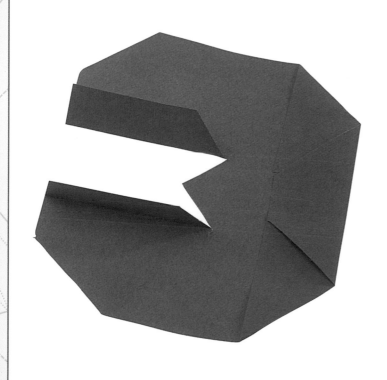

Lay a 3 x 3 sticky note sheet adhesive side up and find the centerline. As shown in Fig. 9-A, fold the two corners in toward the center on the dashed lines. Leave space along the centerline.

Fig. 9-A

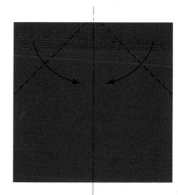

The adhesive will hold the folds in position. Next, on the dashed line in Fig. 9-B, fold the front forward.

Fig. 9-B

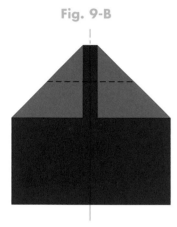

This fold should line up neatly with the two side folds, as seen in Fig. 9-C. Make sure all creases are sharp. The adhesive will hold it together.

Place 3 or 4 small pieces of cellophane tape across the nose for

Fig. 9-C

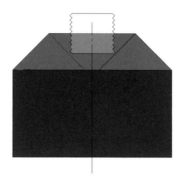

physical balance. Fold the tape around the leading edge of the saucer shape.

Now, look at Fig. 9-D, you are viewing the aircraft from the bottom.

Cut away the rear corners as shown and discard. Make a "Y"-shaped cut up the centerline starting at the rear, then bend the fins up along the dashed lines.

Fig. 9-D

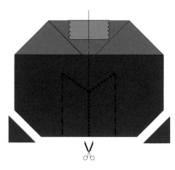

Fig. 9-E shows the saucer from the front. Note that the fins are canted inward.

Fig. 9-E

forward view

Use launch method #3. Experiment with both a little dihedral and anhedral. An interesting, futuristic flyer.

Vader

Size: 3 x 3
Class: Cut
Type: Deep Delta

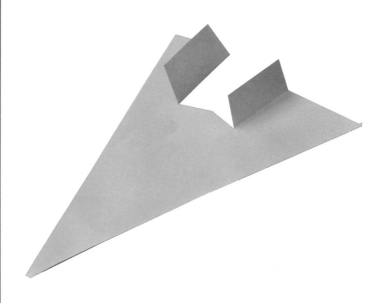

Take a 3 x 3 sticky note sheet and find the centerline. With the sheet flat, fold the right corner with the adhesive along the dashed line, *past* the centerline, as in Fig. 10-A.

Fig. 10-A

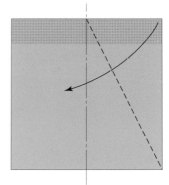

Now fold the left corner on the dashed line as in Fig.

10-B and around the wing edge as in Fig. 10-C. The adhesive will hold the folds. You are viewing the aircraft from the bottom. Keep the creases sharp.

Fig. 10-B

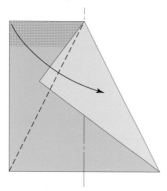

Fig. 10-C

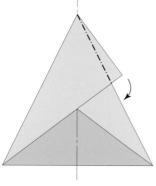

You now want to view the aircraft from the top. Turn the aircraft over so that it looks like Fig. 10-D. You'll see that there's some overlap from the other side, but that's okay! It doesn't affect the plane's flying ability one whit.

Fig. 10-D

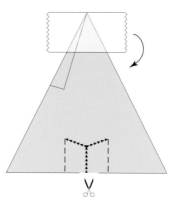

Add about 4 pieces of tape as shown and fold them to conform to the nose. Make a shallow "Y" cut starting

at the back and up the centerline. Then fold the fins up along the dashed lines. The top of the "Y" will be the elevator. It may not look very impressive seen head on, in Fig. 10-E, but what you now have is a miniature Lord Vader Star Destroyer.

Fig. 10-E

forward view

Because of the deep delta design, this ship will fly fast. Use the elevator as needed for trim, and send "Vader" into hyperdrive with launch method #3.

Diamondback

Size: 3 x 3
Class: Cut
Type: Split Fuselage

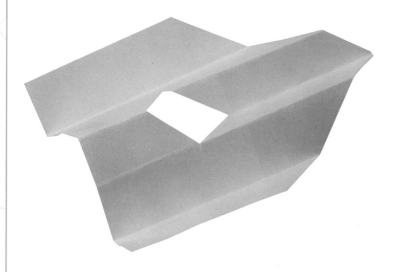

Take a 3 x 3 sticky note sheet with adhesive side up and find the centerline. As shown in Fig. 11-A, fold each adhesived corner into the centerline.

Fig. 11-A

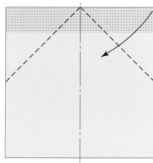

The adhesive will hold the folds in position. In Fig. 11-B, you are viewing the aircraft from the bottom. Fold it along the centerline to the back, as shown by the arrow.

Fig. 11-C

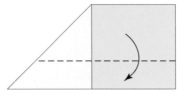

side view

Fig. 11-E

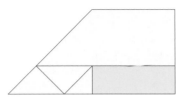

Fig. 11-B

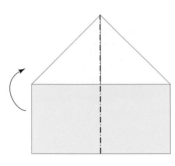

The first folds will be on the *outside*. Orient the form as in Fig. 11-C, and fold downward on the line shown.

As shown in Fig. 11-D, fold the wing upward again on the dotted line.

Fig. 11-D

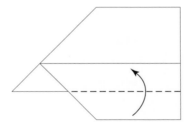

A line from the first fold can also be seen in Fig. 11-E. Now, make the last two wing folds on the other side of the aircraft.

Once you have matching folds on each side, unfold the wings so the aircraft looks like Fig. 11-F from the side. Cut away and discard the section shown.

Fig. 11-F

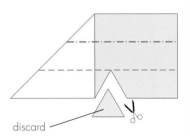

discard

Remake the wing folds but fold the cut aft section upward, so that it appears as shown in Fig. 11-G.

Fig. 11-G

Add about 3 or 4 pieces of tape to the nose, and launch using method #3.

By expanding or contracting the wing sections, see the Fig. 11-H view from the front, you will be able to change speed and stability characteristics.

Fig. 11-H

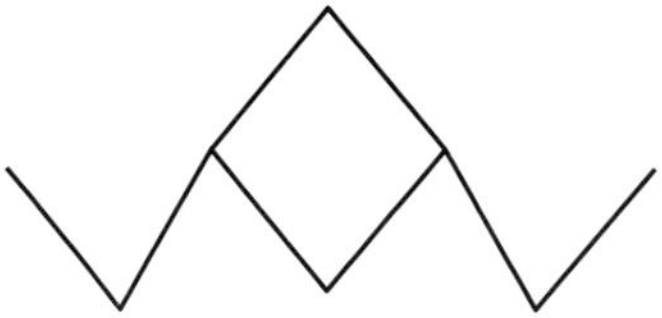

forward view

B-2

Size: 3 x 5
Class: Cut
Type: Wing

Find the centerline of a 3 x 5 sticky note sheet, then lay it down with the adhesive side up as in Fig. 12-A. Fold the corners down on the dashed lines.

Fig. 12-A

The result should look like Fig. 12-B on the next page. There you are viewing the aircraft from the bottom.

Fig. 12-B

Turn the aircraft over and add three pieces of tape to the nose as shown in Fig. 12-C. Fold the tape under the leading edge, then fold the wing upward along the centerline.

Fig. 12-C

overhead view

Cut away and discard the back portion of the wing, as shown in Fig. 12-D.

Fig. 12-D

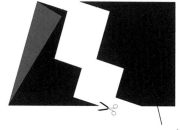

cut and discard

side view

Open the wings until you have only a slight dihedral, as seen from the front in Fig. 12-E.

Fig. 12-E

forward view

Using launch method #3, *gently* send the aircraft forward.

This aircraft has a long wingspan compared to the length of its fuselage. It is therefore affected by even the slightest change in balance. You'll find it a challenge to make this aircraft fly.

Once again, this aircraft demonstrates why we need computers to make the microsecond by microsecond decisions needed to monitor the stability of a plane like the real B-2 bomber. Though the "flying wing" design has been around for years, it has been a problem. It is efficient, provides a means for a high payload, and presents the smallest head-on target, but it is inherently unstable. Only the constant monitoring of stability by dedicated computers has allowed this concept to finally prove itself.

Swift

Size 3 x 5
Class: Cut
Type: Bird

Lay a 3 x 5 sticky note sheet adhesive side up. Find the centerline, then fold the corners forward on the dashed lines, as shown in Fig. 13-A.

Fig. 13-A

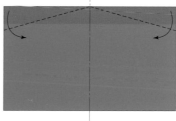

The adhesive will hold the folds in position.

Fig. 13-B

In Fig. 13-B, you are viewing the aircraft from the top. Fold the sheet on the centerline.

Orient the aircraft as in Fig. 13-C, then cut through both wing layers as shown.

Fig. 13-C

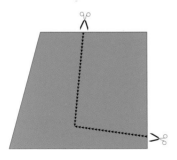

side view

Discarding the cut sections, fold the wing tips forward along the dashed line. Now fold the wings forward along the lower dashed line to form a keel. Make the creases sharp.

Fig. 13-D

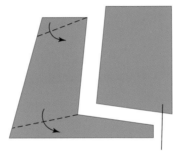

discard

Open the wing folds so the aircraft looks like Fig. 13-E as viewed from the front.

Fig. 13-E

forward view

You will need about three pieces of tape across the nose for trim. Notice that the keel hangs down in the rear. The flight path will follow the wing attitude, *not* the keel. The aircraft's normal flight resembles a bird like a swift or a tern in a slow steady glide. Raising or lowering the wing *tips* will give needed directional trim.

Use launch method #1.

Cutlass

Size: 3 x 3
Class: Cut
Type: Swept/Tailless

Lay a 3 x 3 sticky note sheet adhesive side up. Find the centerline, then fold the corner on the dashed line, as shown in Fig. 14-A, *across* the centerline.

Fig. 14-A

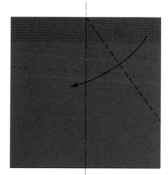

Make a similar fold on the opposite side, as shown in Fig. 14-B. The adhesive will hold the folds.

Fig. 14-C

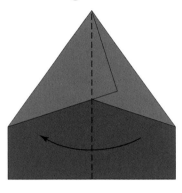

Fig. 14-B

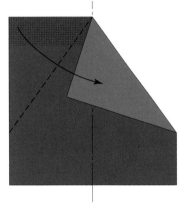

In Fig. 14-C, you are viewing the aircraft from the bottom. Fold the aircraft in half along the centerline, wings downward.

Reorient the aircraft to the side. Cut away a section as in Fig. 14-D.

Make an additional small cut into the wing section as shown to form rudders, and fold them to each side.

Fig. 14-D

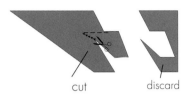

cut   discard

side view

Open aircraft as shown in Fig. 14-E. Add about 3 or 4 pieces of tape to the nose and bend to conform with the leading edge.

Fig. 14-E

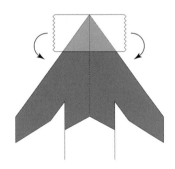

overhead view

As seen in Fig. 14-F, the aircraft will have a slight anhedral.

Fig. 14-F

forward view

Any flight trim adjustments are made on the outer wing panels. Use launch method #3 and pay close attention to balance. This is a fast flyer!

Sticky Note Two-Stage

Each of the following designs is constructed using two sticky note sheets. One is used for the wings and one for the fuselage and tail section. There are four complete aircraft, along with diagrams for two additional wings. These wings and fuselages can be utilized in a "mix & match" format to combine various flight characteristics. Each finished airplane will exhibit different results regarding speed, time aloft, distance, and control. The planes are all pretty much novelty designs, but they are definitely engaging.

V-Plane ■ **Reach** ■ **Delta** ■ **2 DI**

Wing Variations

V-Plane

Size: 3 x 3 (2 sheets)
Class: Two-Stage
Type: V-Tail

Lay a 3 x 3 sticky note sheet with the adhesive side up and positioned to the right as shown in Fig. 15-A. Fold the sheet in half on the dashed line as shown by the arrow. The adhesive will hold the fold.

Fig. 15-A

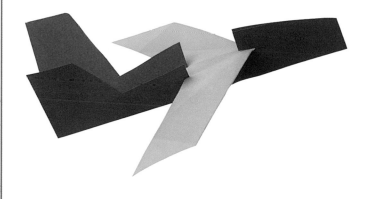

This is the start of the aircraft fuselage. The front of the aircraft is oriented to the right. As shown in Fig. 15-B, cut away the upper portion shown. Extend the sides of the lower cut for the wing.

Take another 3 x 3 sticky note sheet and find the centerline. Lay it with the adhesive side up as in Fig. 15-C. Cut away the lower section, and fold both corners on the dashed lines as shown by the arrows.

You are viewing the wing from the bottom. Turn it over and *carefully* insert it into the cuts made in the fuselage, as shown in Fig. 15-D. You will have to curve the wing from front to back to fit.

Fig. 15-B

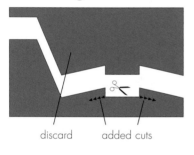

discard   added cuts

side view

Fig. 15-C

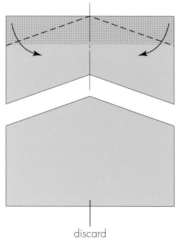

discard

Fig. 15-D

The lower cut should be curved. It may also be adjusted to accommodate different wings. Set the fuselage aside.

Spread the rear section of the aircraft into a "V" as in Fig. 15-E.

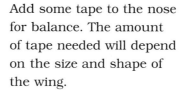

Fig. 15-E

forward view

Add some tape to the nose for balance. The amount of tape needed will depend on the size and shape of the wing.

Remember, wings are interchangeable. Balance *first*, then trim for flight.

Use launch method #1.

Reach

Size: 3 x 3 (2 sheets)
Class: Two-Stage
Type: T-Tail

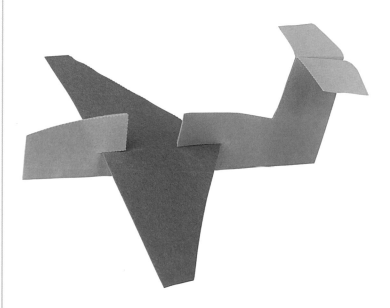

Lay a 3 x 3 sticky note sheet with the adhesive side up and positioned to the right as shown in Fig. 16-A. Fold the sheet upward, in half, on the dashed line as shown by the arrow. The adhesive will hold the fold.

Fig. 16-A

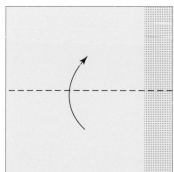

This is the start of the aircraft fuselage. The front is to the right. With the folded sheet oriented as in Fig. 16-B, cut away portions as shown.

Add two lower cuts to accommodate the wing; don't forget to curve. (The cuts may be adjusted for different wings.)

Lay a *small* piece of tape across the lower leading edge of the rudder, as shown, to keep it together. Fold the rear wings at the dashed lines and position them to form a "T." Give the rear wings a little dihedral. Set the fuselage aside.

· · · · · · · · ·

Lay another 3 x 3 sticky note with the adhesive side up as shown in Fig. 16-C. Fold the section of sticky with the adhesive forward on the dashed line.

The adhesive will hold the double-thick wing. Find the centerline, *without* folding. Shape the wing by cutting away the lower portion as shown in Fig. 16-D.

You are viewing the wing from the bottom. It has the edge of the fold.

Fig. 16-B

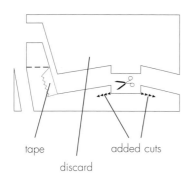

tape   added cuts

discard

Fig. 16-C

Fig. 16-D

discard

Turn the wing over and *carefully* insert it into the cuts made in the fuselage. You will have to curve the wing from front to back to fit. The view from the front should resemble Fig. 16–E.

Fig. 16-E

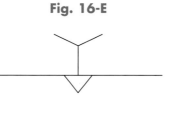

forward view

Start with 3 or 4 pieces of tape on the nose for balance. Use care when applying trim to the rear wings as they are sensitive. Use launch method #1.

Delta

Size: 3 x 3 (2 sheets)
Class: Two-Stage
Type: Tailless

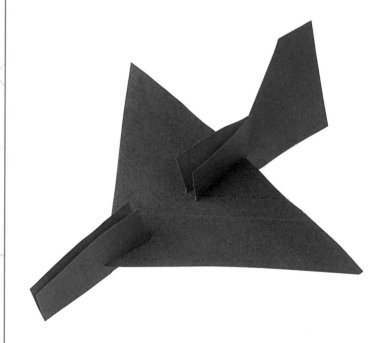

Lay a 3 x 3 sticky note sheet with the adhesive side up and positioned to the left, as in Fig. 17-A. Fold the sheet upward, in half, on the dashed line as shown by the arrow, using the adhesive to hold.

Fig. 17-A

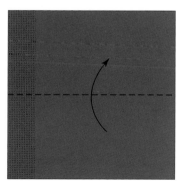

The front of the aircraft fuselage is to the right. With the folded sheet in position, cut away the portion shown in Fig. 17-B.

Fig. 17-B

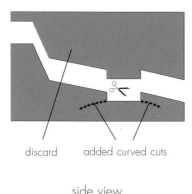

discard   added curved cuts

side view

In this aircraft, the adhesive holds the rudder closed. Make the lower curved cuts for the wing. (Note: This cut may be adjusted for different wings but will be deepest for the Delta.) Set the fuselage aside.

. . . .

Lay another 3 x 3 sticky note sheet with the adhesive side up as shown in Fig. 17-C. Find the centerline and fold each adhesived corner as shown. Cut away and discard the lower portion.

Fig. 17-C

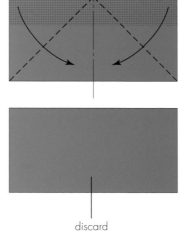

discard

You are viewing the wing from the bottom. Turn it over and *carefully* insert it into the cuts made in the fuselage as shown in Fig. 17-D. You will have to curve the wing from front to back to fit.

Fig. 17-D

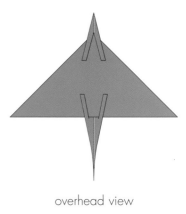

overhead view

Fig. 17-E

forward view

Add tape to the front for balance. The amount of tape needed will depend on the size and shape of the wing. Remember, wings are interchangeable. Balance *first*, then trim for flight. For this aircraft, use launch method #1.

2 DI

Size: 3 x 3 (2 sheets)
Class: Two-Stage
Type: Standard

Lay a 3 x 3 sticky note sheet with the adhesive side up and to the left, as in Fig. 18-A. Fold the sheet upward, in half, on the dashed line as shown.

Fig. 18-A

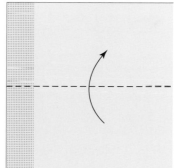

The front of the aircraft is to the right. The rear is held by adhesive. Cut away the portion shown in Fig. 18-B. Make lower curved cuts to accommodate the wing. Note: This cut may be adjusted for different wings.

Fig. 18-B

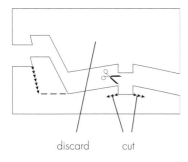

discard   cut

Make another cut near the tail and fold both sides on the dashed line for smaller rear wings. Set the fuselage aside.

Lay another 3 x 3 sticky note sheet with the adhesive side up as shown in Fig. 18-C. Fold the entire adhesive edge over on the dashed line to form a double layer.

Fig. 18-C

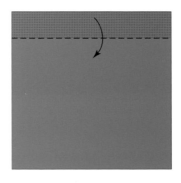

Cut away and discard the lower portion. In Fig. 18-D you are viewing the wing from the bottom.

Fig. 18-D

discard

Turn the wing over and *carefully* insert it, as shown in Fig. 18-E, into the cuts made in the fuselage. You will have to curve the wing from front to back to fit. The wing tips fold upward.

Fig. 18-E

Fig. 18-F

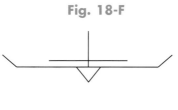

forward view

Remember, wings are interchangeable. Balance *first*, then trim for flight. Use launch method #1.

Add tape to the front for balance. The amount of tape needed will depend on the size and shape of the wing.

Position the wing tips and back wings as shown in Fig. 18-F.

On the following pages are instructions for two additional wing variations.

It is worth mentioning again that the ability to mix and match different wings and fuselages in the Two-Stage section will yield many more aircraft than actually shown. Each combination will give different flight performance results regarding glide path, speed, time aloft, and accuracy.

Adjusting the cut for main wing placement and static balance is critical to any kind of flight, and trim adjustments on rear wings are very sensitive because of the fragile aspect of the rear wings.

Once static balance and correct trim are established, these planes fly well and will elicit a chuckle because of their strange appearance and good flight characteristics.

1

Lay a 3 x 3 sticky note sheet with the adhesive up as in Fig. 19-A.
Fold the entire adhesive section down as shown.

Fig. 19-A   **Fig. 19-B**

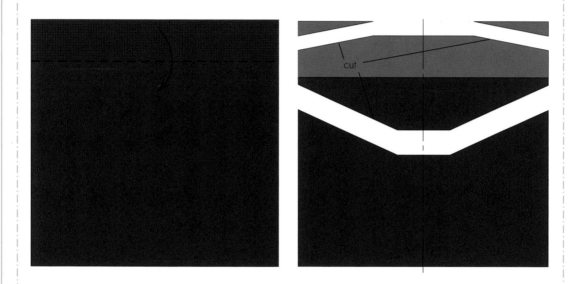

The adhesive will hold the double layer. Cut away the sections as shown in Fig. 19-B for a
different wing shape. As much as possible, make the wing ends match (symmetrical).

2

Lay a 3 x 3 sticky note sheet with the adhesive up as in Fig. 20-A.
Fold the entire adhesive section down to form a double layer.

Fig. 20-A   **Fig. 20-B**

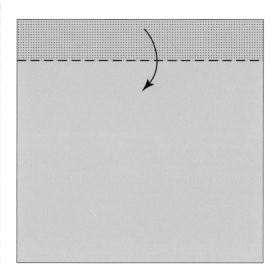

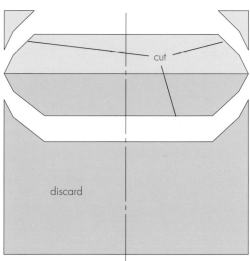

With the adhesive section at top, cut away the portions shown in Fig. 20-B. This pattern produces a wider air contact area for better support.

Sticky Note Concepts

The following designs use single sheets of 3 x 3 or 3 x 5 sticky notes. Their form is unorthodox or unusual; however, their design theories are sound. Take a few moments to think through their flight characteristics and the result will be an aesthetically pleasing, fine-performing aircraft.

Simplex ■ Manta ■ Vector ■ A-12 ■ Air Sled ■
Cruise 1 ■ Condor ■ Spirit

Simplex

Size: 3 x 3
Class: Concept
Type: Simple Wing

Lay a 3 x 3 sticky note sheet with the adhesive side up, as in Fig. 21-A. Find the centerline, but *do not crease*. Fold both adhesived corners in toward the center as shown.

Fig. 21-A

The adhesive will hold the folds. In Fig. 21-B, you are viewing the aircraft from overhead. Lay about 3 or 4 pieces of tape across the nose as shown. Fold the tape edges downward.

Fig. 21-B

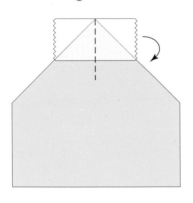

overhead view

Now, put a light crease in the *forward area only* along the centerline, causing a slight dihedral in the nose as shown in Fig. 21-C.

Fig. 21-C

Do not continue the crease all the way back. The aircraft is roughly balanced. Using launch method #3, send the aircraft gently forward. If it noses up or "porpoises," add another strip of tape.

If the aircraft heads abruptly down, remove one layer of tape. If it should bank sharply to either side, trim correction is required at the rear of the wing panel. Any easy bank will result in the aircraft attempting to right itself. This is an automatic control factor caused by the built-in dihedral. Final flight path should be a level, straight (or easy banked) float at slow to moderate speed.

Manta

Size: 3 x 3
Class: Concept
Type: Anhedral Wing

Lay a 3 x 3 sticky note sheet with the adhesive side up. Find the center-line, as in Fig. 22-A, but *do not* crease. Fold the corners up on the dashed lines and join the adhesived tips.

Fig. 22-A

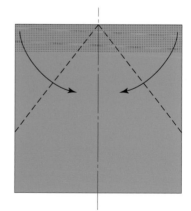

Extend the join to the nose of the aircraft and angle it so the sweep of the wing extends slightly over halfway toward the rear of the aircraft, as shown in Fig. 22-B.

Fig. 22-B

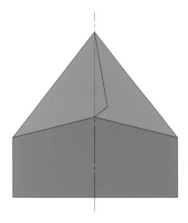

Make the creases sharp. The aircraft is now lying top down, with its short keel facing up. The adhesive should be holding the keel and the upper/lower wing surfaces together. Viewing the aircraft from the bottom, in Fig. 22-C, cut away the pieces as shown.

Fig. 22-C

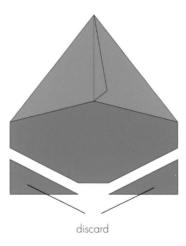

discard

Turn the aircraft over and lay about four pieces of tape across the nose, as shown in Fig. 22-D. Fold the tape to conform to the leading edge.

Fig. 22-D

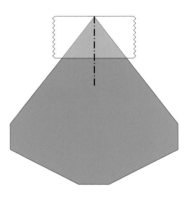

overhead view

Add anhedral, as shown in Fig. 22-E. Bend the wings down and make a short and slight crease on the centerline, *only as far as the keel.*

Fig. 22-E

forward view

Make *all* trim adjustments in *small* increments. Trim directionally with the outwing panels, and nose up and down with the rear elevator.

Use launch method #1 or #3. Aircraft should fly nearly level and float.

Vector

Size: 3 x 3
Class: Concept
Type: Vent Wing

Lay a 3 x 3 sticky note sheet with the adhesive side up. Find the centerline but *do not* crease. Bring each adhesived corner across the centerline. Find the dashed fold line shown in Fig. 23-A, and *press lightly*. This will be only a slight, *not* sharp, crease.

Fig. 23-A

Move the adhesived corners back across the centerline. Position them to each side, as in Fig. 23-B. This will produce a space or gap between the upper and lower wing surfaces. The adhesive will hold the slightly rounded wings.

In Fig. 23-C you are viewing the aircraft from the bottom. Cut away the sections shown and fold the wing tips toward you on the dashed lines. Turn the aircraft over.

Fig. 23-D shows the aircraft from the top. Start with about four pieces of tape for balance. Gently fold them over to conform to the nose and wings.

Fig. 23-B

Fig. 23-C

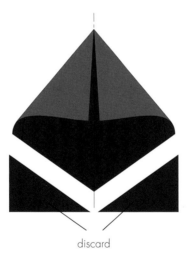

discard

Fig. 23-D

overhead view

Fig. 23-E shows the aircraft from the front. Note that the aircraft will have a slight anhedral.

Fig. 23-E

forward view

Any flight trim adjustments are made on the outer wing panels. Use launch method #3 and pay close attention to balance. Be prepared for unusual performance.

A-12

Size: 3 x 5
Class: Concept
Type: Stealth

Lay a 3 x 5 sticky note sheet with the adhesive side up. Find the center-line, as in Fig. 24-A, but *do not* crease. Fold the corners with adhesive on the dashed lines from the top center to the lower right and left corners.

Fig. 24-A

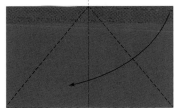

The folds will reach past the centerline, as in Fig. 24-B, and the adhesive holds the crease. Make these creases sharp.

Fig. 24-B

You are now viewing the aircraft from the bottom. Turn it over and lay about 6 pieces of tape across the nose, folding the tape edges down as in Fig. 24-C.

Fig. 24-C

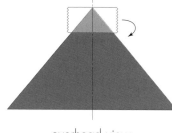

overhead view

View the aircraft from the front and put a shallow crease in the nose. This causes the wings to bend slightly anhedral as in Fig. 24-D. *Do not* continue the crease all the way back.

Fig. 24-D

forward view

Using launch method #3, you will find that the aircraft wants to spin right. (If you reverse the folds, it will want to spin left.) You will need to trim, bending the right panel down. You may also need to center up. Add or remove tape to balance.

. . . .

This planform closely approximates a stealth-type wing; and you can now understand why the pilot needs computer help to maintain control. After some trial and error, you will find this aircraft's flight performance great.

Air Sled

Size: 3 x 3
Class: Concept
Type: Vectored Wing

Lay a 3 x 3 sticky note sheet with the adhesive side up and find the centerline as in Fig. 25-A, but *do not* crease. Fold the adhesive section forward on the dashed line, as shown, to form a two-layered section.

Fig. 25-A

Along the new leading edge, find a point about half the distance between the centerline and outer right side of the aircraft. Fold inward along the dashed line as shown in Fig. 25-B.

Fig. 25-B

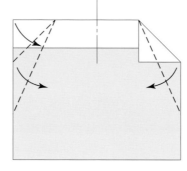

From that same leading edge point, make another fold on the dashed line to a point further down the right wing panel, as

shown in Fig. 25-C. Repeat the two folds on the opposite side. Make all creases sharp.

Fig. 25-C

Add 2 or 3 strips of tape to the nose, as shown in Fig. 25-D, and fold the tape under. You may need to add even more tape for weight.

Fig. 25-D

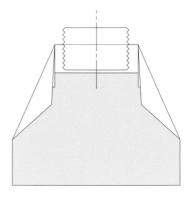

The folds are on the top of the aircraft. Open the longer, second wing folds until the panels stand nearly vertical, as shown in Fig. 25-E.

Fig. 25-E

forward view

The front of the aircraft now has channeled air dams that slow flight and provide better stability. By raising or lowering these dams, you will create more or less drag on a given side and will be able to control speed and direction.

Using launch method #3, send the aircraft forward. Trim as needed for level flight. Correctly balanced, this aircraft flies slow and stable.

Experiment with some different air dam settings and check their effect on flight performance.

Cruise 1

Size: 3 x 3
Class: Concept
Type: Double Delta

Lay a 3 x 3 sticky note sheet with the adhesive side up. Find the centerline but *do not* crease. Cut along the solid lines, as shown in Fig. 26-A. Fold the cut parts forward, toward the centerline, on the dashed lines.

Fig. 26-A

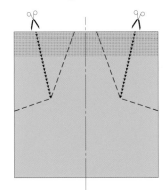

With the folds, the bottom view of the aircraft should look like Fig. 26-B.

Cut away the sections shown. The adhesive should hold the folds (add *small* pieces of tape to help if needed). Turn the aircraft over.

Fig. 26-B

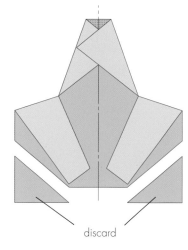

discard

Fig. 26-C shows the aircraft from the top and the position of the tape. Start with 3 or 4 pieces of tape on the nose for balance. Gently fold them to conform smoothly with the wing's leading edge. Bend the wings downward with a very slight crease on the centerline.

Fig. 26-C

overhead view

Note that the aircraft, as in Fig. 26-D, has only a very slight anhedral.

Fig. 26-D

forward view

Any flight trim adjustments are made on outer wing panels. Use launch method #3 and pay close attention to balance. This plane just looks "nasty" as it flies.

Condor

Size: 3 x 5
Class: Concept
Type: Wide Vectored Wing

Lay a 3 x 5 sticky note sheet with the adhesive side up and find the centerline. As shown in Fig. 27-A, fold on the dashed line from the top center to the lower part of the adhesive at the outer wing panel.

Fig. 27-A

Next, fold that same corner on the dashed line, as shown in Fig. 27-B, from about the center of the previous fold to a point about halfway down the remaining outer wing panel.

Fig. 27-C

Reopen the aircraft and add tape to the nose. Start with about three strips, and gently fold under to conform to the leading edge of the wing.

Fig. 27-B

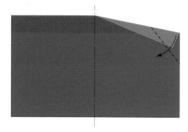

Fold the aircraft in half on the centerline. Cut away and discard the sections as shown in Fig. 27-D.

Fig. 27-E

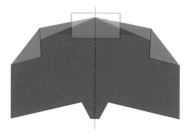

overhead view

Fig. 27-D

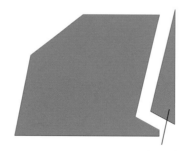

discard

side view

Repeat the fold pattern on the other side so the aircraft looks like Fig. 27-C. You are viewing the aircraft from the top.

Give the aircraft a slight dihedral and raise the two secondary folds of the wing to nearly vertical, as shown in Fig. 27-F, for air dams.

Fig. 27-F

forward view

Although this aircraft has both "cut" and "concept" properties, it falls into the "concept" section by virtue of its controls.

Using launch method #3, send the aircraft forward. Once it is trimmed so it does not dive or stall (porpoise), its side-to-side stability or "yaw" can be controlled by raising or lowering the air dams. Banks and spins can be controlled by outer-wing panel adjustment. Properly trimmed, this aircraft flies slow and stable with a fairly high glide ratio.

Spirit

Size: 3 x 5
Class: Concept
Type: Reverse Delta Wing

Lay a 3 x 5 sticky note sheet with the adhesive side up. Fold the top right corner forward to the lower left corner of the sheet, as shown in Fig. 28-A, and crease at the fold line.

Fig. 28-A

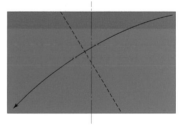

Essentially, that's it. The adhesive will hold the fold. Remember, sharp crease. Orient the aircraft as in

Fig. 28-B and decide
which is to be the top
and bottom.

Fig. 28-B

Find the centerline
and very lightly crease
the nose for a slightly
anhedral wing orientation.
Fig. 28-C shows the
location of the tape for
trim weight.

Fig. 28-C

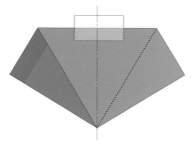

Start with four pieces of
tape; you will probably
need more. Assuming you
are looking at the top of
the aircraft, gently "curve"
the wing *tips* upward, as
seen in Fig. 28-D. The
rear-pointed elevator is
for up/down trim.

Fig. 28-D

Use launch method #3.
This anhedral wing
aircraft is sensitive to
force of launch (be gentle)
and it will also tend to
"yaw" without banking. It
almost seems alive as it
floats. Balance and trim
are both critical, but well
worth the effort as you see
Spirit fly.

Accessories

Paper clip stand (see Figs. Q and R)

Some models work out so well that they just *can't* be thrown away. You can display them as desk references easily by opening a paper clip as shown and sliding the selected aircraft onto the raised stem. You may need a piece of tape to secure it.

Fig. Q

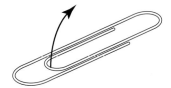

Fig. R

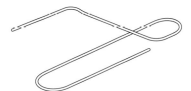

Wastebasket (see Fig. S)

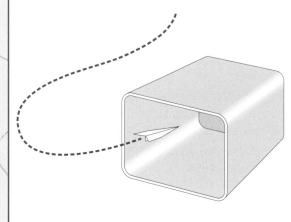

Fig. S

This accessory is invaluable for several reasons:

1. When laid down as shown, it's a perfect target area, and when you're finished...no clean up! Just turn the wastebasket back upright.
2. It provides instantaneous storage in case you have devoted "too much" time to your new activity (and the boss is coming).
3. As a target area, it provides a fair standard for performance measurement.
4. Most of these things are going to wind up there anyway...

Ideas and Notes

Here's where you get to dream a little...

Index

A-12, 107–108

accessories, 121–122

aeronautic forces, 13-14

Airfoil, 55–56

Air Sled, 109–111

anhedral, 22

B-2, 66–67

balance, 14–16, 91

classes, Sticky Note
  airplane
    Classics, 25–37
    Concepts, 95–120
    Cut, 49–73
    Fold, 39–48
    Two-Stage, 75–93

Condor, 115–117

control surface, 15

Cruise 1, 113–114

Cutlass, 71–73

Cylon, 57–58

Dart, 27–29

Delta, 85–87

design categories, 17

Diamondback, 61–63

dihedral, 22

display, 121

drag, 13–14

F-15, 51–53

Flash Gordon, 31–33

folding symbols, 16

forces, primary, 13-14

glide ratio, 14–15

gravity, 13, 14

kinetic balance, 14–15

launch methods, 19–20

lift, 13–14

Manta, 99–101

needed items, 15

Orbiter, 47–49

Reach, 81–83

Simplex, 97–98

Spirit, 119–120

SST, 35–37

Swift, 69–70

thrust, 13

trim, 20–21

2 DI, 89–91

U Lite, 41 43

Vader, 59-60

Vector, 103–105

V-Plane, 77–79

weight, 20

wing variations, 92–93

About the Author

STEVE SCHMIDT, born and raised in the Chicago area, is a military veteran of the Viet Nam era. His education and pursuits include a Bachelor of Arts Degree in Music Education, and schooling in the fields of electronics and aviation. Life experiences include work in technical customer service management, computer video, teaching, and as a performing musician; plus membership in a civic association involved with the preservation of Meigs Field in Chicago; the design and construction of flying model aircraft, and physical fitness.

Although Steve Schmidt's writing interest centers on short stories, the vast majority of his school teachers, albeit reluctantly, can attest to the talent that led to this particular publication. He has made *many* paper airplanes....